N
W
E
S
W0259683
GLASSFORD
STREET
N
W
E
S

PLACES

IMPORTANT SITES IN BLACK BRITISH HISTORY

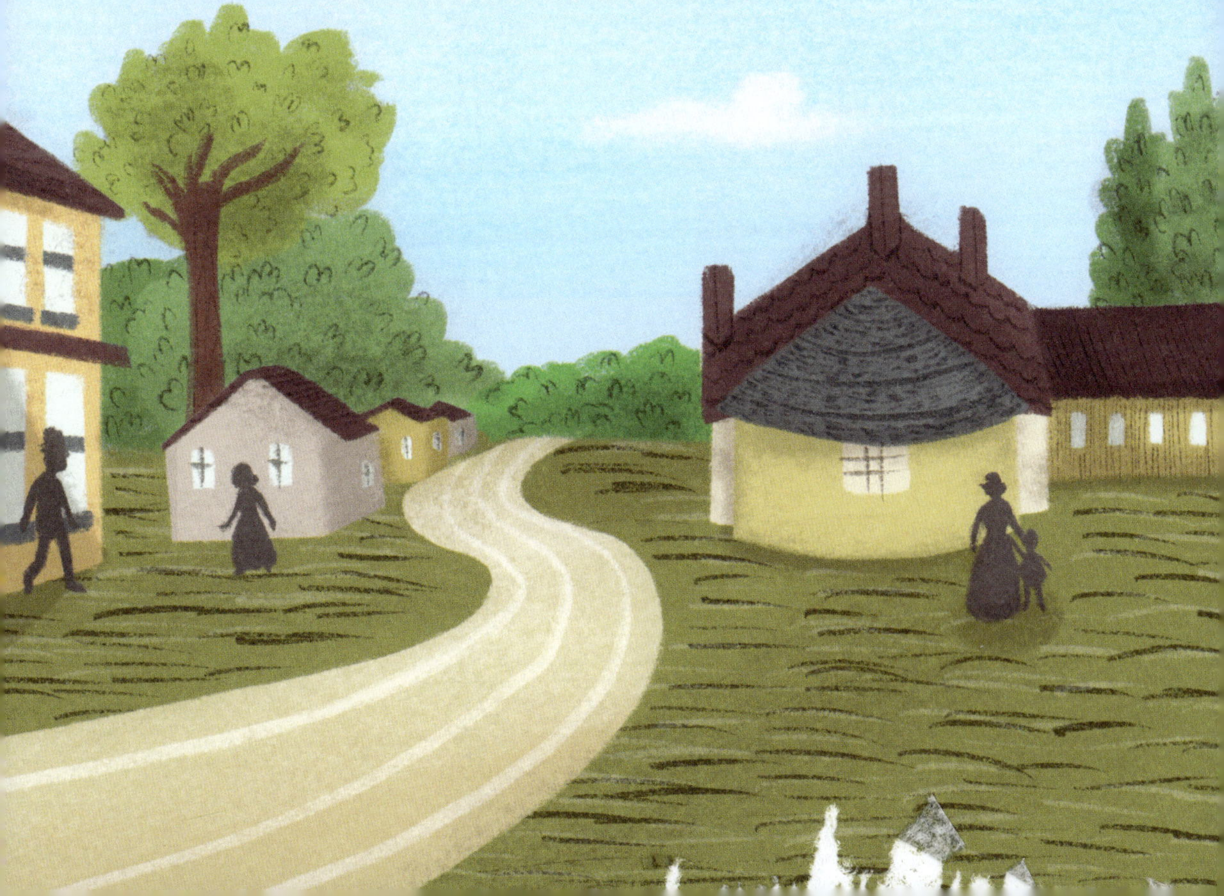

We are so thrilled that you are reading The Black Curriculum's first books! It means so much to us as a team, and I hope that these books inspire you to dive into your passions, hopes, and dreams. Go be great!

LAVINYA STENNETT, FOUNDER AND CEO OF THE BLACK CURRICULUM

The Black Curriculum is an organisation dedicated to promoting the learning of Black British history in and out of schools.

PLACES

IMPORTANT SITES IN BLACK BRITISH HISTORY

WRITTEN BY
MELODY TRIUMPH

ILLUSTRATED BY
AMANDA QUARTEY

Contents

Arthur Roberts (Page 28)

Florence "Rosie" Parris (Page 43)

FREE THE CARDIFF THREE

CHAPTER 2: WALES

CHAPTER 3: ENGLAND

Princess Campbell
(Page 61)

John Ystumllyn
(Page 36)

Timeline

In this book you will read different stories from Black British history, across different places in Britain. Here are a few key dates placed in order of when they happened.

208

EMPEROR LUCIUS SEPTIMIUS SEVERUS
arrives in Britain.

1400s

THE TRANSATLANTIC SLAVE TRADE
starts in the 1400s.

1509

JOHN BLANKE
performs at both Henry VII's funeral and Henry VIII's coronation.

1824

JOHN EDMONSTONE
moves to Edinburgh by 1824 and works for the University of Edinburgh's zoological museum.

1833

The Slavery Abolition Act 1833 abolishes slavery throughout the British Empire.

1846

FREDERICK DOUGLASS
gives speeches in Edinburgh. His most famous one takes place at the Assembly Rooms in 1846.

1913

JOHN ARCHER
becomes the first Black mayor in London.

1919

Tiger Bay Riots of 1919.

IRIS DE FREITAS BRAZAO
begins her studies at Aberystwyth University in 1919. She goes on to become the first female lawyer in the Caribbean.

1948

WINDRUSH

1959

AN INDOOR CARIBBEAN CARNIVAL TAKES PLACE AT ST PANCRAS TOWN HALL, Jan. 1959
Organised by activist Claudia Jones, this event is believed to be the precursor to the Notting Hill Carnival.

1963

Bristol Bus Boycott in 1963.

Britain is most involved with the Transatlantic Slave Trade between 1640 and 1807.

Carnivals first start in Trinidad and Tobago.

1640 **1700s** **1784**

GEORGE AFRICANUS moves to Nottingham and starts a business and a new life.

Slavery is banned in most of the British Empire in 1807.

Carnival celebrations are banned in Britain.

1807 **1800s**

BRITISH BLACK PANTHER MOVEMENT 1968-1973

CLIVE SULLIVAN plays in the 1975 Rugby League World Cup.

1966 **1968** **1969** **1975** **1988**

The Caribbean Artists Movement (CAM) is founded in London in 1966.

CECILE YVONNE CONOLLY CBE becomes Britain's first female Black head teacher.

NAOMI CAMPBELL becomes the first Black model to feature on the cover of French *Vogue*.

Foreword
by Darcus Beese

Did you know that Betty Campbell was the first Black head teacher in Wales and that she worked at Mount Stuart Primary School? Did you know that Clive Sullivan was the first Black sports captain for Britain? Did you know that North Africans helped to build Hadrian's Wall? No? Neither did I. In fact this book is packed full of fascinating facts and stories that I would have cherished at your age.

You see, I grew up in the 1970s at a time when we didn't learn about Black British history in school. Everything I knew about our history, I learnt from my parents, Darcus Howe and Barbara Beese, both of whom were political activists who were determined to instil in me a sense of pride and belonging. In 1971, they were part of the Mangrove 9, a group of activists who were arrested and charged for protesting against police brutality. They were acquitted in a ground-breaking court case where the judge, for the first time in British history, acknowledged there was racism in the Metropolitan Police.

This solid grounding and sense of identity gave me the confidence and tools to be successful in the music industry, and I became the first Black president & CEO of a major record label. So much of our history sits within the walls and streets of the UK; inspiring stories that celebrate people and places where history has been made. From Glasgow to Cardiff, and from Bristol to London; my home town.

One such place that is special to me is 173 Railton Road. It was the HQ of the Race Today Collective, an organisation that fought for equal rights and justice, and a place where I spent much of my childhood watching and learning as my parents stood up against racism.

I recently returned to the site for the unveiling of a blue plaque for my father Darcus Howe, the Black activist, writer, and broadcaster. Eighteen years earlier in the exact same spot, I attended a similar ceremony for my uncle CLR James, the pioneering writer, historian, and activist. It makes me incredibly proud to know that their legacy will live on, as new generations walk by and are inspired to find out who the people behind those blue plaques are.

Reading the Tiger Bay story, I was reminded of the moments in my early life when I was a witness to key events that helped to change the course of our history. Sometimes I was watching from the sidelines, but often I was centre stage as I walked proudly with my banner at the front of many demonstrations. I remember the Black People's Day of Action when thousands of young people took to the streets of London to protest the racist attack that led to the tragic death of 13 young teenagers in a house fire in New Cross. I stood alongside my dad as we bellowed slogans of freedom from the truck – it was a sad, but triumphant day that I will never forget. On that day, I was part of making history.

As time and communities move on, it's important to mark those significant events so that our stories, our achievements, and our struggles are not forgotten. Be that in the name of a building, in the words of a song, or in a book like this. Most importantly, we need to remember that we can all play a part, however big or small, in shaping our future and our story.

My dad used to say, "You only know who you are when you understand where you have come from." I've always been curious about our past and drawn inspiration from those that have gone before me. I hope the stories within these pages do the same for you and encourage you to keep reading and learning. With knowledge comes confidence, and with confidence you can achieve your dreams.

Introduction

Have you ever read a book, watched a film, or heard a story that you liked, but didn't feel fully included?

A lot of the time, when people try to learn about **Black British history**, all the stories they hear are from **London**. For example, we hear about the bookstore **New Beacon Books in Finsbury Park**. Or the Black Victorian classical composer **Samuel Coleridge-Taylor** who was brought up in Croydon. We may even hear about **Notting Hill Carnival** which came out of the Notting Hill race riots, or the **Windrush monument** at Waterloo station.

Black British history in London is really **important** to learn, but we also need to remember that London isn't the only place in Britain! London makes up a small part of Britain, which means Black British history in London is only a section of all the **Black history in Britain**.

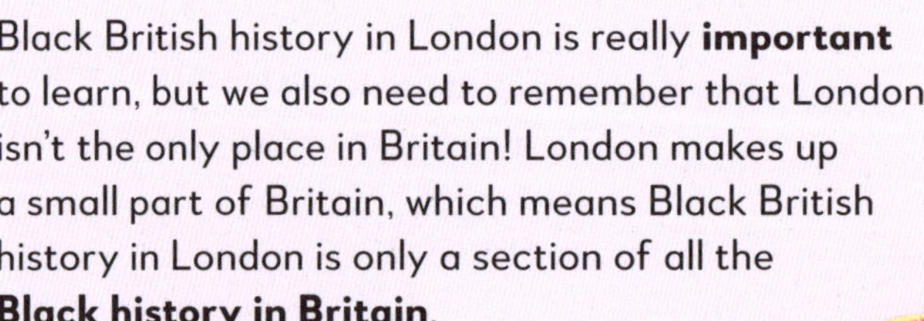

There is Black history in Wales, in Scotland, and so much Black history in Northern Ireland that it would need a whole separate book!

There is also Black history in England, in places outside of London, like **Bristol**, **Leeds**, **and Nottingham!** Britain is full of stories about Black British history just waiting to be told.

You will even have undiscovered histories in London itself. For example, you may have heard of **Mary Seacole**, a Black Victorian nurse, who was born in Kingston, Jamaica. She learnt all about nursing in Jamaica then came to London and helped soldiers in the Crimean war. However, you may not have heard about **Sarah Forbes Bonetta**, who was an African orphan during the Victorian times, and was looked after by **Queen Victoria and became her goddaughter**!

If you didn't know about that in London, imagine all of the **wonderful stories**, events, and places linked to Black British history all over Britain that **you have never heard of**.

This book will be the start of learning about just a handful of Black British stories from all over Britain.

We are going to look at different people you may not have heard of, different events you may not know about in your own city, and different places that are full of Black British history.

All the way through the book, there will be **activities and questions** I'd like you to have a think about and take part in. **Why?** Because learning about **YOUR local Black British history is so important**! Remember the question I asked at the beginning? Have you ever read a book, watched a film, or heard a story that you liked but **didn't feel fully included**? A lot of us feel that way, because we are often talking about British history that **does not include us**.

It is up to all of us to dig deep and find those wonderful stories about Black British history that often go unnoticed.

We do this by **reading books** like this, **asking family and friends**, looking at **museums and libraries**, and choosing to be interested in the **history of Black people in Britain**.

This book is just the beginning of an **exciting journey** and **adventure** about Black British history in different parts of Britain, and hopefully, with your help, we will find a lot more Black British history in **different places and spaces all over Britain**.

SCOTLAND

Skye

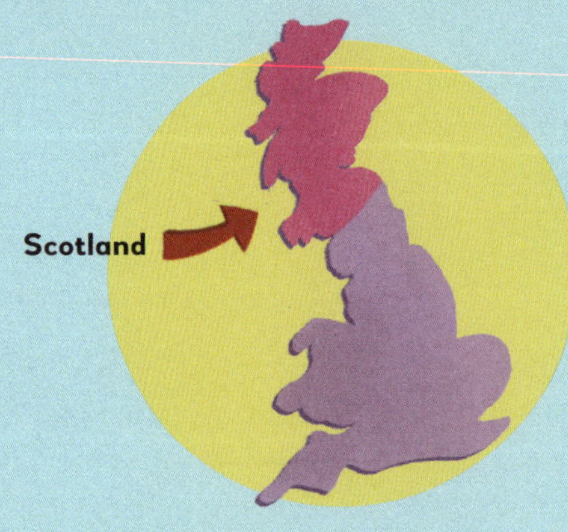

HEBRIDES

Isle of Mull

Labrador Sea

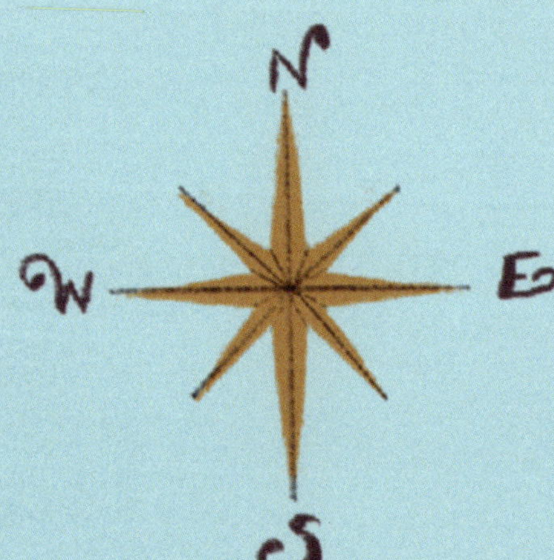

Islay

Isle of Arran

Wick
Nairn
Elgin
Cairngorms National Park
Aberdeen
Loch Lomond
Arbroath
Dundee
North Sea
Perth
Stirling
Glasgow
Edinburgh

Black British History in Scotland

We are going to start our journey by learning about Black British history in Scotland.

Scotland is known for its bagpipes, kilts, the amazing Highlands, and the mythical creature, the Loch Ness Monster.

Scotland is also known for having early arrivals from the Roman Empire. In Roman times, troops from North Africa built Hadrian's Wall along the border between England and Scotland.

So as early as the Roman Empire, there have been Africans in Scotland! However, the history doesn't stop there. Records show there were also Black people who worked as servants for King James IV of Scotland, who ruled from 1488-1513. There were also Black musicians and choreographers in Edinburgh.

The Transatlantic Slave Trade

The Transatlantic Slave Trade started in the 1400s.

People from different countries in Europe, including Portugal, France, and Spain, would go to African countries and swap items like gold, ivory, and spices for enslaved African people. Europeans used tactics such as waging war and pitting communities against each other in order to manipulate people in West Africa into selling others into slavery. Other times, people were captured by the Europeans in coastal raids and sold into slavery.

Europeans would then sell enslaved Africans to people in America and the Caribbean to work as slaves on plantations producing items like sugar, cotton, or tobacco. These items were taken to European countries and sold to people living there.

The Trade Triangle

The Transatlantic Slave Trade is sometimes known as the Triangular Slave Trade. This is because of the journey that European ships would make. The ships would make three stops.

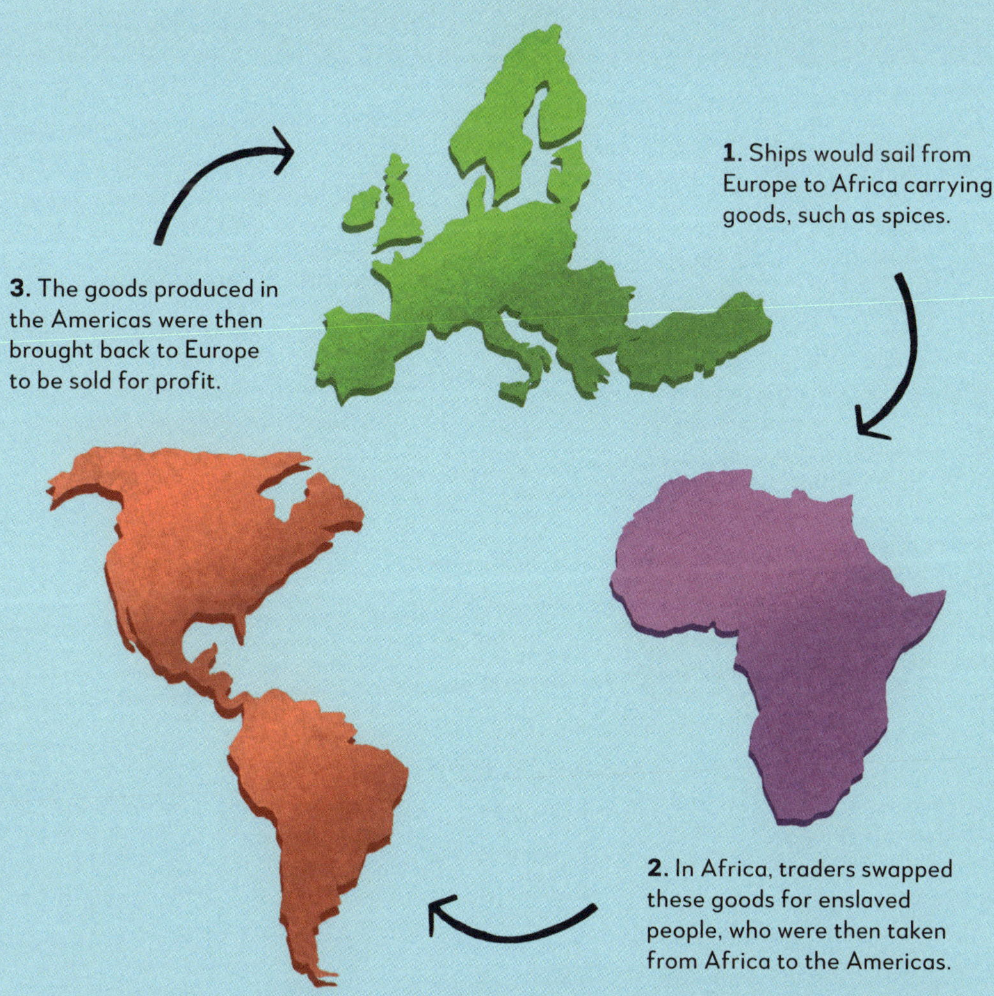

If we draw this out on a map, it makes a triangle shape, so it has become known as the Triangular Slave Trade.

Goods

Here are some examples of goods that were traded or sold for profit during the Transatlantic Slave Trade. Some, like cotton and sugarcane, were grown by enslaved people in the Americas.

Spices
These are things like cardamom, which can be used in cooking.

Gold
This is a very valuable material often used to make jewellery.

Cotton
This is a plant that can be used to create textiles and clothing.

Tobacco
People would have used this to either smoke or chew.

Sugarcane
This plant is used to make sugar, to sweeten food.

Ivory
This material is made from elephant tusks.

Street Names

Evidence of the history of the Transatlantic Slave Trade can still be found all over modern-day Britain, including in Scotland. For example, in Glasgow, many streets are named after people or places who were connected to the slave trade.

Ingram Street

This street was named after Archibald Ingram. He made his fortune through tobacco plantations that used the labour of enslaved people.

Glassford Street

This street was named after John Glassford. He was a wealthy tobacco baron who owned plantations in Virginia and Maryland in the US.

Kingston Bridge

This street was named after Kingston, Jamaica, to celebrate Scottish merchants' trade links in the Caribbean (meaning their links to the slave trade).

Life in Britain

Britain was most involved with the Transatlantic Slave Trade between 1640 and 1807. During this time, Black people arrived in Britain for many reasons, and they had different experiences of living here.

Some came because they had been enslaved and arrived from the Caribbean with their enslavers. This is not the only reason Black people came to Britain at this time, however. Some were students from West African countries like Sierra Leone. Some came willingly as free people working as sailors on the slave ships. The experience of living as a Black person in Britain at this time would have been very different for different people. Many lived and died as enslaved people. However, many others lived as business people, musicians, or had other professions.

Before the slave trade was banned in Britain in 1807, Black people in Britain had a wide range of different experiences. Even people living freely would have had to deal with racial prejudice and poverty.

They might have sought out education themselves in the hope of moving up in society. Or, they might have been sent to learn new skills by the people they worked for. They would have gone to places like Jock's Lodge in Edinburgh. For example, an enslaved man called Joseph Knight went there to learn how to cut hair. Since many Black people were there, they would also use it as an opportunity to socialise.

Learning new skills at a place like Jock's Lodge would be beneficial to the person themselves, as well as the people they worked for.

Frederick Douglass

The African American writer, slavery abolitionist, and speaker Frederick Douglass would come to Edinburgh and Glasgow in the 1840s to speak against the Transatlantic Slave Trade.

In 1846, he came to Glasgow after speaking in Ireland. For a long time, Glasgow relied on the slave trade to support its economy. Frederick Douglass made speeches in Glasgow criticising the Free Church of Scotland, who accepted donations from American enslavers.

Frederick Douglass' journey to Scotland

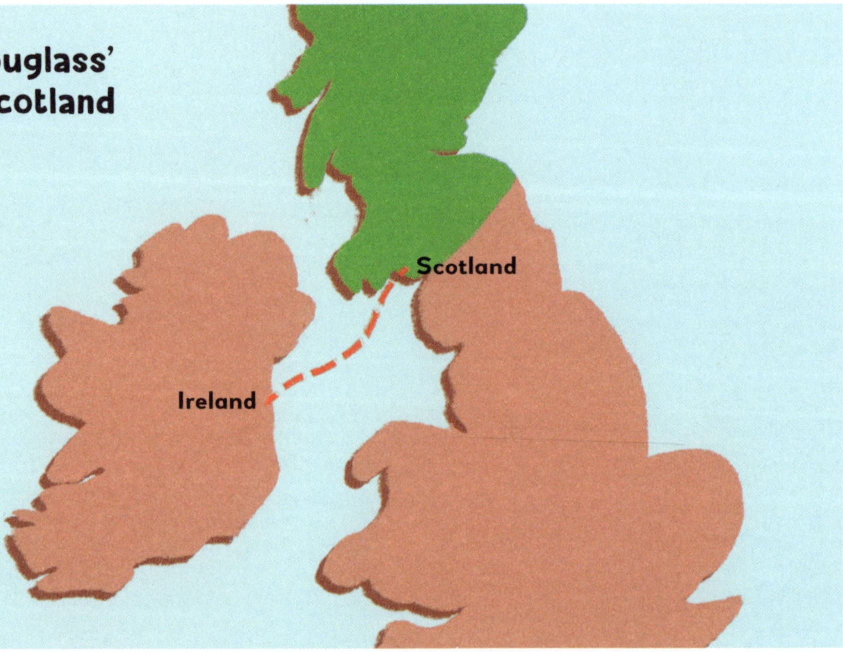

Scotland

Ireland

Douglass arrived in Scotland via a ship from Ireland.

Frederick Douglass also made speeches in Edinburgh. One of his famous speeches happened at the Assembly Rooms in 1846. A huge crowd listened as he told the true story of an enslaved man called Madison Washington who fought for his freedom. Douglass told this story to get people to side with the cause of abolishing slavery.

John Edmonstone

You might not have heard this name before. But without John Edmonstone, Charles Darwin might not have developed his Theory of Evolution.

John Edmonstone was an enslaved man from Guyana. He took his last name from Charles Edmonstone, the man who enslaved him, and came to Scotland with him in 1817. However, owning slaves in Scotland was banned in 1778 after the famous case of James Knight.

James Knight was an enslaved person who won his freedom by challenging the courts and suggesting that slavery did not exist in Britain under common law. So, when John Edmonstone came to Scotland, he was automatically a free man on Scottish soil.

At first, John Edmonstone lived in Glasgow but had moved to Edinburgh by 1824. He worked for the University of Edinburgh's zoological museum and lived at 37 Lothian Street. He learned about taxidermy, which is when people preserve animals by stuffing them.

The naturalist Charles Darwin hired John Edmonstone to teach him about natural history. Edmonstone taught Darwin about taxidermy. Thanks to his lessons from John Edmonstone, Darwin was able to preserve the species of birds he found on his travels. This was important because it helped Darwin study the birds and develop his Theory of Evolution. This theory changed science forever.

John Edmonstone practising taxidermy.

John Edmonstone's story is amazing, especially because we don't often hear about the brilliant Black British science that shaped history.

Charles Darwin and John Edmonstone.

Arthur Roberts and World War I

John Edmonstone's story is not the only unheard story in Scotland. There is also the story of the soldier Arthur Roberts, whose diaries were discovered almost 100 years after he wrote them.

Have you ever heard of Arthur Roberts? If you haven't, don't worry! It is very rare to find a first-hand account of World War I from the many Black soldiers who helped Britain. However, we do have the story of Arthur Roberts. Roberts was born in Bristol, before moving to Glasgow.

After a short period of training in Glasgow, Roberts was sent to France. His diary entries consist of his personal experiences of the different drills, tasks, marches, and his time on the front line. He spoke about his exhaustion and the horrors and injustice of the war. It was clear he felt strongly for Britain and was a patriot.

After the war, he came back to Glasgow, married, and worked as an engineer and electrician. He died in 1982.

For years, Roberts' diaries, photos, and drawings were lost in the attic of a house in Glasgow. When a couple moved into the house in 2004, they discovered the diaries. Arthur Roberts' accounts of World War I give us a powerful insight into what life was like in the trenches.

See What You Can Find Out!

Do you know of any other Black history that happened in Scotland?

Maybe you can ask the adults in your family or your teachers about the Black Scottish history that they know, or stories that were passed on to them. You could also go to the library or online and see what you can find out.

Here are some examples of what you could look for:

See if you can find another **street name** or **place** in **Glasgow** that connects to the **Transatlantic Slave Trade**.

Do you live in **Scotland?** Find out if any adults around you know any interesting facts about Black history in your local area.

How many famous Black Scottish people can you name? They could be writers, actors, sports stars, or musicians.
What can you find out about them?

Wales

Wales
St George's Channel
Fishguard
St Davids
Narberth
Milford Haven
Tenby
Pembroke
Bristol Channel
N
W
E
S

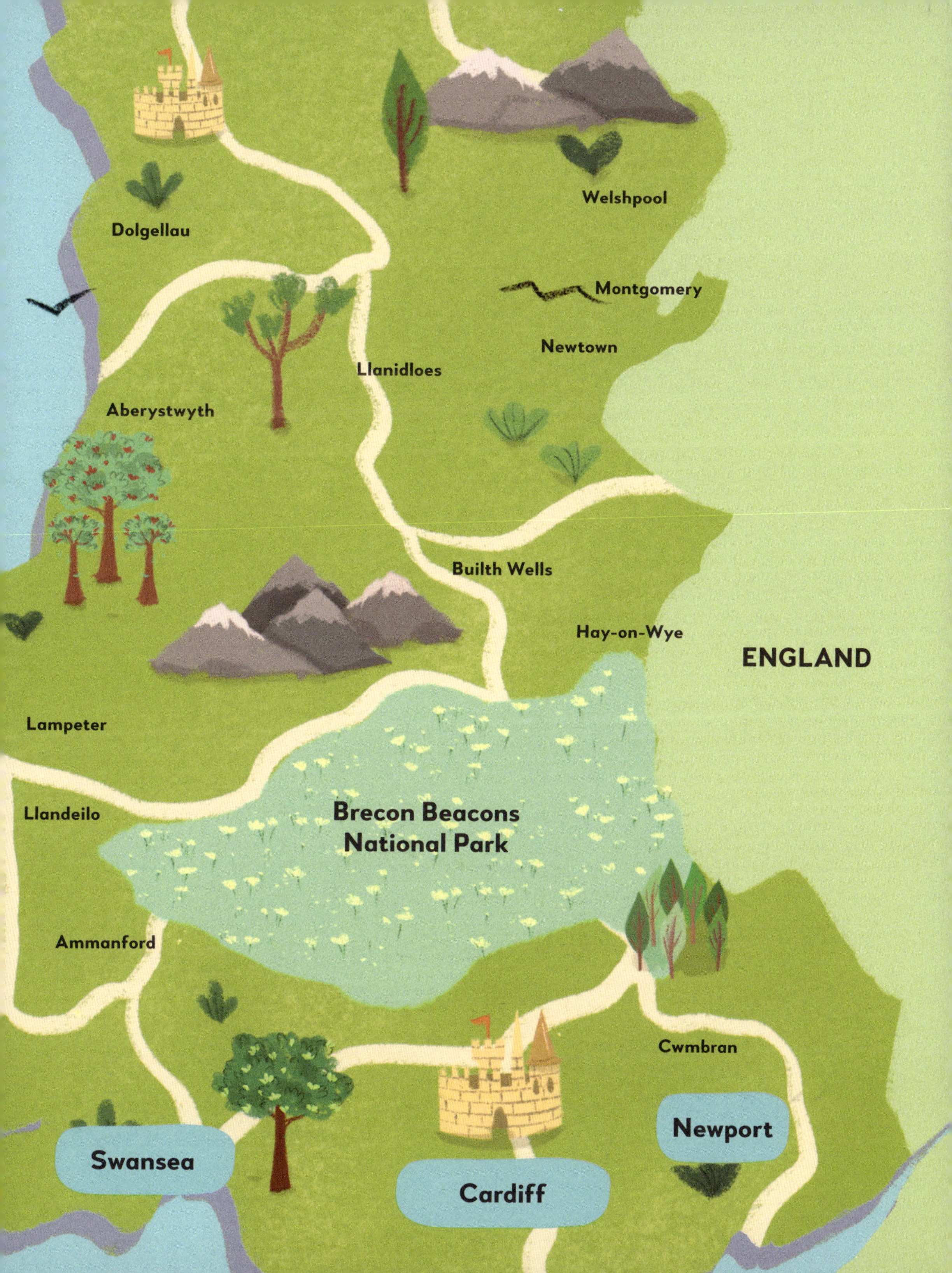

Dolgellau
Welshpool
Montgomery
Newtown
Llanidloes
Aberystwyth
Builth Wells
Hay-on-Wye
ENGLAND
Lampeter
Llandeilo
Brecon Beacons
National Park
Ammanford
Cwmbran
Newport
Swansea
Cardiff

The Transatlantic Slave Trade in Wales

Now we're going to go all the way down to Wales to find out about some Black history there. Just like other places in Britain, a big part of Wales's Black history is tied to the Transatlantic Slave Trade.

Did you know...

...there are more than 200 sites in Wales that reference the Transatlantic Slave Trade?

This includes street names and buildings, as well as statues of people who benefitted from the slave trade and the work of enslaved African people. There are also street names and buildings named after people who fought against the Transatlantic Slave Trade.

Romilly Primary School

Sir Samuel Romilly pub

For example, Picton Terrace in Swansea is named after the plantation owner Sir Thomas Picton. Romilly Primary School, Romilly Avenue, and the Sir Samuel Romilly pub are all named after Sir Samuel Romilly, a lawyer who fought against slavery.

John Ystumllyn

John Ystumllyn is sometimes referred to as the first Black person in Wales. He was, in fact, not the first, but he is notable because of how much we know about his life.

We have seen in this book that the presence of Black people in Britain really started to grow during the Transatlantic Slave Trade. One of the millions of Black people who were taken from Africa and transported to places such as the Caribbean, America, or Britain was John Ystumllyn. He came to Wales in the 1700s.

Even though we do not know his original name, he is often referred to as the first well-recorded Black person in Wales. There were Black people living in Wales before John Ystumllyn arrived. They worked in different jobs including as servants and musicians, and some were landowners. However, we know much more about John Ystumllyn's life than we do other Black people who arrived earlier.

John Ystumllyn's journey to Britain started when he was a young boy. His country of origin is unknown, but we know he was taken from West Africa and arrived in Gwynedd in north Wales. He was given his name when he arrived and was christened, and he started work as a servant for the Wynn family of Ystumllyn estate near Criccieth. John Ystumllyn was taught to speak English and Welsh and how to take care of a garden. John Ystumllyn went on to become a well-known and respected gardener, and the first Black gardener in his area. He also found love and married a local woman named Margaret Gruffydd.

John Ystumllyn left the Wynn family to marry Margaret Gruffydd. After they were married, they lived in Ynysgain Fawr, west of Criccieth. Both of them worked as land stewards taking care of other people's land. John eventually went back to working for the Wynn family. He and Margaret had seven children, and five of them made it to adulthood. There are even some of their descendants alive today and living in the same area where John and Margaret lived in the 1700s!

Tiger Bay Riots of 1919

Many places across Britain have had incidents where fighting has broken out because of racism or another injustice. One incident happened in Tiger Bay, Cardiff.

There have been different kinds of riots, protests, and uprisings in Britain. These events usually happen because a group of people gets tired of something wrong in society. For example, they might be sick of an injustice like sexism or racism. They decide that they have had enough and want to make their voices heard and bring about a change. Sometimes this is done in an organised way, like a protest, but sometimes tensions simply reach a boiling point and fighting breaks out. You might have heard of the Brixton Uprisings in London in 1981, where people clashed with the police because of the racist treatment they received. Or the St Pauls riot in Bristol in 1980, and the Moss Side riots in Manchester in 1981, which were also caused by mistreatment by the police.

An earlier example you might not have heard of is the Tiger Bay riots of 1919.

The story goes:

In 1919, a group of Black men were victims of a racist attack that triggered the riots. White men and women yelled abuse at them in Cardiff centre and many of them became violent towards the Black men. A fight with knives and guns started on Wednesday 11th June and spread across the city centre.

That night, the riot died down but was triggered again on Thursday and continued into Friday. Racist mobs intimidated white women who had non-white partners, homes were attacked and set on fire, and three people died.

Sadly, instead of addressing the racism that had caused the Tiger Bay riots, the British government decided that the solution was to send many of the Black people involved back to the countries they had migrated from.

As a result of the riots, repatriation was seen as a viable option by the British Government, who were terrified of more riots. Hundreds of people were sent from Cardiff Docks to places like Jamaica. The people who had been sent away demanded their repatriation back to Cardiff.

This story is sadly an example of how those in authority have sometimes placed the blame on the wrong people.

Activity

Can you **find out about** another race riot, protest, or uprising that has happened in **Britain?** This could be from the **past** or more recently. Ask your family, teachers, or go to the library or online, and write about what you find out.

Look at the questions below to help get you started:

What were people angry about?
What caused the injustice?
What did people do to stop it?
Who was involved?
Did they achieve their goal?
Did anything change?

Welsh Hall of Fame

Have a look at the Black Welsh people below who have made a great impact on Welsh and British society. Do you recognise any?

Iris de Freitas Brazao

Iris de Freitas Brazao studied Latin, modern languages, law, and jurisprudence (which means different ideas, theories, and opinions about law and how it could work) at Aberystwyth University in 1919. She became the first female lawyer in the Caribbean.

Vivienne A.A.A White MBE also known as: Chalky White

Vivienne was Cardiff's first Black dentist and first Black bus driver. Despite facing racial discrimination, he kept going and also became the first Black youth worker in Wales. He became the head of Race Equality Council Wales and was given an MBE for his work.

Florence "Rosie" Parris

Florence Parris campaigned for the freedom of her brother and two others after they were wrongly found guilty of the murder of Lynette White. They were jailed in 1989, but Florence's constant campaigning and fighting for justice eventually led to their release. It was discovered that police had forced a fake confession out of one of them. Ten years later the real killer – Jeffrey Gafoor – was discovered, and he was put in jail.

The Story of Betty Campbell

We have shown you just a small selection of amazing Black people who have made an impact on Welsh history. Now we are going to look at the story of Betty Campbell, an activist and the first Black head teacher in Wales.

Rachel Elizabeth "Betty" Campbell was born in Butetown in Cardiff. She had a difficult life growing up, experiencing poverty and the loss of her father. She did well in school, winning a scholarship to Lady Margaret High School for Girls, and that's where she decided she wanted to become a teacher.

Betty's scholarship letter from Lady Margaret High School.

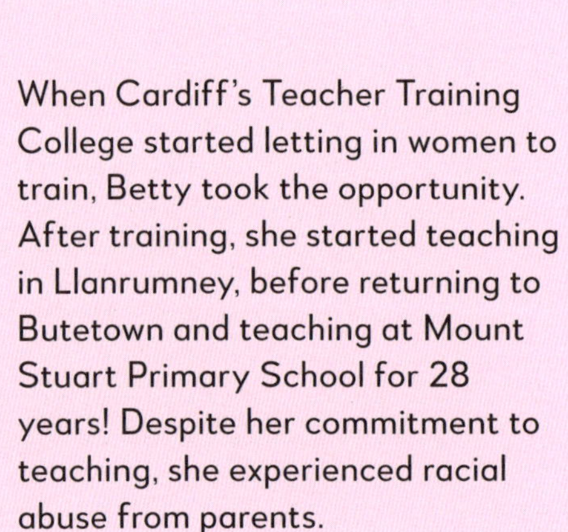

When Cardiff's Teacher Training College started letting in women to train, Betty took the opportunity. After training, she started teaching in Llanrumney, before returning to Butetown and teaching at Mount Stuart Primary School for 28 years! Despite her commitment to teaching, she experienced racial abuse from parents.

Betty was inspired by the American Civil Rights Movement. When she became the head teacher of Mount Stuart Primary School in 1970, she made sure to teach all the children there about Black history.

Betty Campbell met Nelson Mandela in 1988.

She continued her work in teaching and activism. She became a councillor at Cardiff Council and was a member of the Commission for Racial Equality. In 1988, she met Nelson Mandela and she was given an MBE in 2003.

Clive Sullivan: Britain's First Black Sports Captain

Rugby and Wales go hand in hand. The sport is very important to the country. It brings people together, and, amazingly, it is also the sport that had the first Black captain in the whole of Britain.

Clive Sullivan was serving in the army when he first played for Hull FC in 1961.

Clive Sullivan was born in Splott in Cardiff in 1943. He started playing rugby when he was 14, and after school, he joined the army. He was stationed far from Wales in a village called Catterick in Yorkshire, England. When he was there, he was picked for a small rugby match just because he was Welsh!

Clive Sullivan only played a bit of rugby during his time in the army. Then, after leaving the army in 1964, he was able to focus on playing rugby. He played rugby in London, Leeds, Hull, Australia, and New Zealand.

Clive Sullivan played against Huddersfield for Hull FC in 1968.

Clive Sullivan scored an amazing solo try against Australia in the 1972 Rugby World Cup final.

In the 1972 Rugby World Cup, Clive captained Great Britain. He scored a try in each of their games, and team GB lifted the cup.

In the 1975 Rugby League World Cup, Clive Sullivan led Wales in all of their matches. He scored a try in their second game, beating England.

Overall, Clive Sullivan represented Britain 17 times and played at three World Cups, two of them for Britain and one of them for Wales. He also still has two records for Hull – the most tries in any rugby career (250) and the most tries in one match (7 against Doncaster). He is one of only 25 Welsh rugby players to score more than 1,000 points in their Rugby League career.

Isn't that incredible?

Wales Makes History Today!

From **teachers** to **lawyers** and **bus drivers**, we have seen just a small part of the **amazing Black history in Wales**. And it doesn't stop there! Even though it had a history with the Transatlantic Slave Trade (like a lot of the places we have seen), in recent years Wales has made a lot of effort to become more and more **inclusive**.

Betty Campbell (Head Teacher)

Iris de Freitas Brazao (Lawyer)

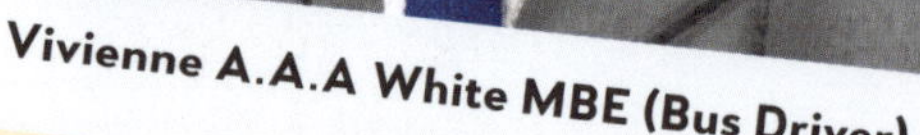

Vivienne A.A.A White MBE (Bus Driver)

Wales will be **MAKING more Black British history**, because it will be the first place in Britain to make sure all children learn about Black history in school. This means that you might end up learning about all the places we looked at today, and more!

Activity

Write or **draw** any ideas of the kind of **Black Welsh history** you want to **learn** about in school and even some ways you could make that happen!

England

Liverpool

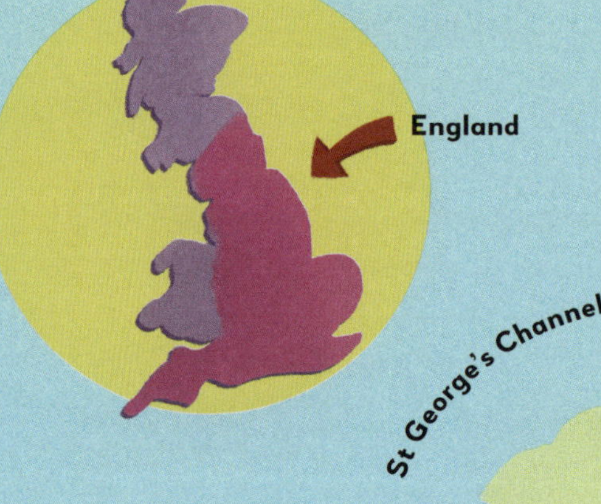

St George's Channel

WALES

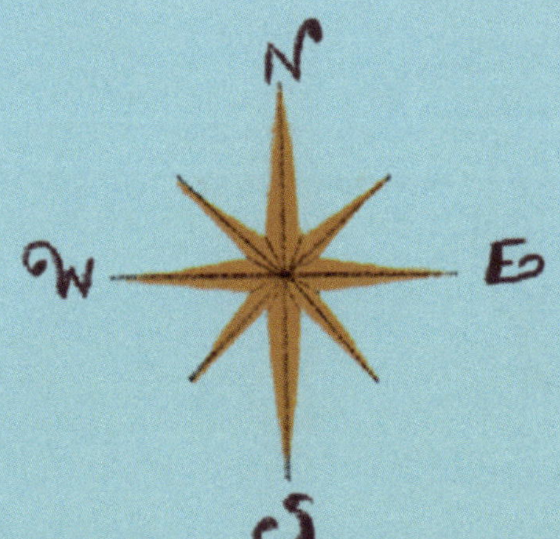

Bristol Channel

Bude

Exeter

Leeds
Hull
North Sea
Manchester
Nottingham
Derby
Leicester
Peterborough
Norwich
Birmingham
Coventry
Worcester
Cambridge
Ipswich
Colchester
Oxford
THE BAMBOO CLUB
Reading
London
Bristol
Canterbury
Southampton
Brighton
Bournemouth
English Channel

Black British History in Bristol

Welcome to Bristol! We are going to look a little bit more at the places and spaces where Black British history and art, music, and culture connect in Bristol.

People in Bristol came together to protest the "colour bar" in 1963.

Like other places in Britain, Bristol was linked to the Transatlantic Slave Trade. As a busy port, ships carrying enslaved people would often arrive in Bristol. Later, during the Bristol Bus Boycott in 1963, many Black and South Asian people avoided using the bus service as a protest against the "colour bar". This was an unspoken rule that banned or made it really difficult for Black people and other people who weren't white to use public transport, and get good jobs or housing.

However, it is important to also learn about the Black history related to the arts and music in Britain. That is why, in this chapter, we are going to look at the culture Black people brought to Britain and Bristol.

Black people have made amazing contributions to Britain's music scene.

The Sounds of Bristol

When Black Jamaicans migrated to Britain during the 1950s and 1960s, they made sure to bring their music with them. It was a way to stay connected with their life in Jamaica and also create a sense of community in their new home in Britain.

The racism people experienced in Britain during this time meant that these Jamaicans couldn't enjoy their music and dance in the clubs and dance spaces that were already there. So, many Jamaicans became creative and made their own spaces to dance. These were often called "shebeens".

The Bamboo Club opened in 1966 and was a hub of the community until it sadly burned down in 1977.

These nights were often held in basements, for example, Ajax in St Pauls. This helped sound system culture (a musical culture and genre from Jamaica featuring DJs playing music on turntables) to grow. Nights were also held in more formal clubs like the Dockland Settlement and the Bamboo Club – which is famous for having Bob Marley and the Wailers, Desmond Dekker, and Tina Turner perform there!

Bob Marley and the Wailers performed at the Bamboo Club in 1973.

Have you ever heard of reggae, dub, or ska? These are other types of Jamaican music that influenced the music in Bristol. DJs and pirate radio stations (meaning unofficial radio stations, legal or illegal) allowed people to hear these new and underground sounds that weren't played on popular radio stations.

St Pauls Carnival

Carnival celebrations started in the Caribbean and were brought to Britain when people migrated. Today, Carnival is enjoyed all over Britain, including St Pauls in Bristol.

Many of the carnivals we see in Britain are related to the Caribbean. It is agreed by many that Caribbean carnivals started in Trinidad and Tobago (an island in the Caribbean) in the late 18th century, during the time of European colonialism. After the abolishment of slavery in 1833, many previously enslaved Black people turned Carnival into a time they could use to dress up, dance, play music, and celebrate themselves and their culture.

During the 1800s, the British government tried to stop the new celebrations by creating laws to ban them. Traditional stick fighting, which was a big part of Carnival, was banned, and parties needed a licence. However, despite the efforts to stop it, Carnival is still a big part of Afro-Caribbean culture. Many Black Caribbeans who migrated to Britain took this culture of Carnival with them to places like Notting Hill in London and St Pauls in Bristol.

Carnival has its roots in celebration, and in St Pauls, Carnival was originally known as St Pauls Festival. It was started as a way of bringing together different European, African, Afro-Caribbean, and South Asian cultures. Over time, it was known as St Pauls Carnival and then in 1991 it was renamed to be St Pauls Afrikan Caribbean Carnival as a way of making sure the Afro-Caribbean influence on the event was recognised.

Activity

Have a think about the history of Carnival and the different types of Carnival across Britain. There is Notting Hill Carnival (started by Claudia Jones) in London, which is one of the biggest carnivals in the world; Manchester Caribbean Carnival; Leeds West Indian Carnival; and Birmingham Carnival. Are some of these places near you? What can you find out about them?

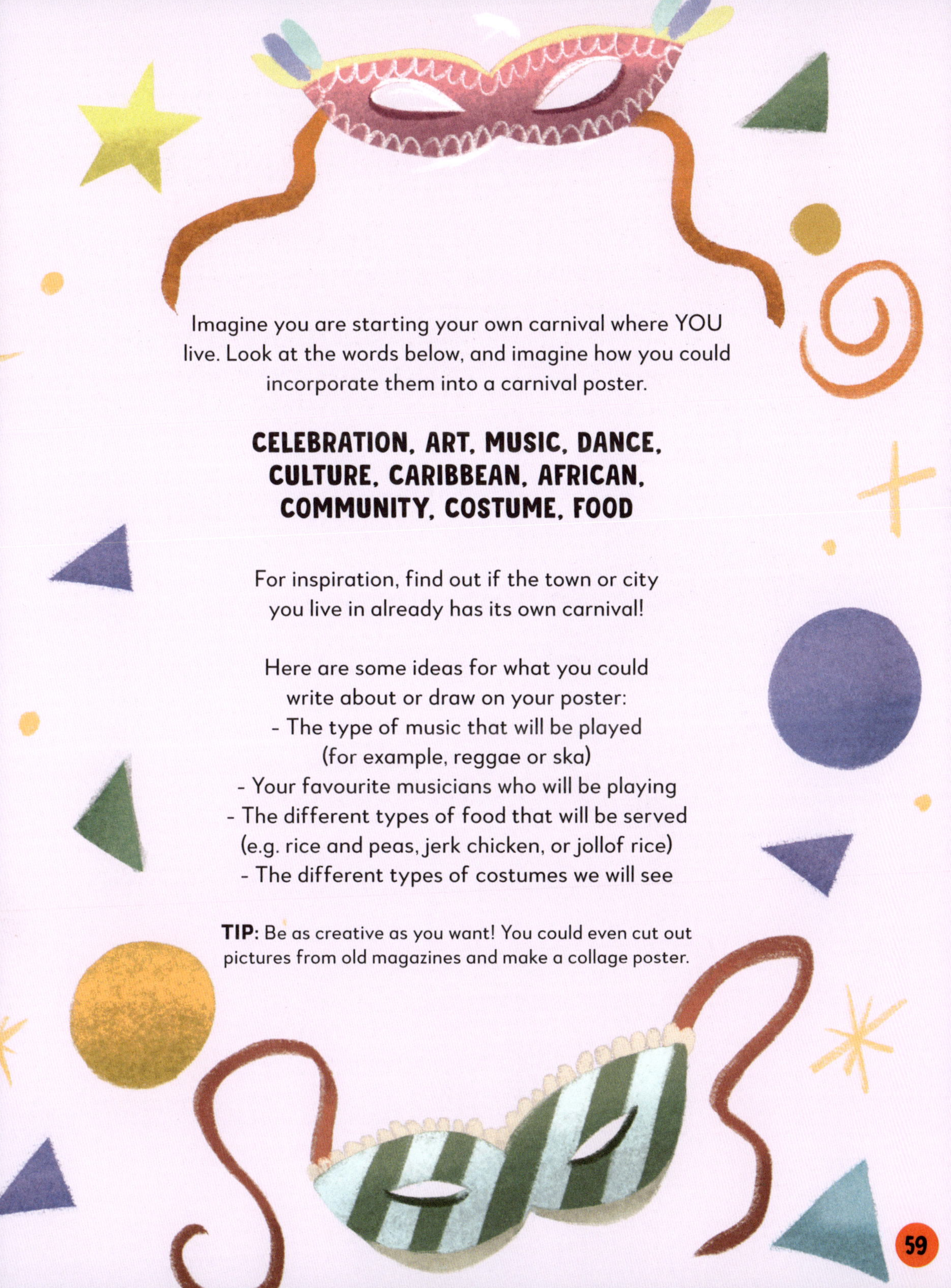

Imagine you are starting your own carnival where YOU live. Look at the words below, and imagine how you could incorporate them into a carnival poster.

CELEBRATION, ART, MUSIC, DANCE, CULTURE, CARIBBEAN, AFRICAN, COMMUNITY, COSTUME, FOOD

For inspiration, find out if the town or city you live in already has its own carnival!

Here are some ideas for what you could write about or draw on your poster:

- The type of music that will be played (for example, reggae or ska)
- Your favourite musicians who will be playing
- The different types of food that will be served (e.g. rice and peas, jerk chicken, or jollof rice)
- The different types of costumes we will see

TIP: Be as creative as you want! You could even cut out pictures from old magazines and make a collage poster.

The Black Women who Shaped Bristol

It's important to make sure that when we look at Black British history, we are being as inclusive as possible. A lot of the time, people from marginalised groups, such as Black women, are not included in books – even books celebrating Black history. So, we are going to have a look at some amazing Black women who shaped Bristol's Black history.

Carmen Beckford MBE

Carmen Beckford was born in Jamaica and went to school there. When she came to Bristol, she played a very important role in starting the first St Pauls Carnival. She also did a lot of positive work in her community and became the first Black person to get an MBE in the South West of England. She was also Bristol City Council's first community development officer, which also made her the first Black person to work in a high position in the city. She did an amazing job and a lot of important work in helping to fight against racism in Bristol.

Hyacinth Hall MBE

Did you know that by 2018, there had only been 26 Black head teachers out of 1,346 in Bristol? Hyacinth Hall was Bristol's first ever Black head teacher. She became the first Black head teacher and was the head of St Barnabas school in St Pauls. Whilst she was teaching, Hyacinth pushed against poor teaching standards for Black students. She was given an MBE in 2004 for her work against racism in education and the community.

Princess Campbell MBE

Princess Campbell was one of the first Black nurses in the NHS in Bristol. She campaigned for many disadvantaged communities in Bristol and took part in other community organisations and groups to celebrate Black history. She was very important in leading the way against racial discrimination in nursing and housing. She received an MBE for all her amazing work in 2011.

Alfred Fagon

Alfred Fagon was born in Jamaica in 1937 and arrived in England in 1955. He started his life in Britain in Nottingham, where he worked on the railways. He joined the army in 1958 for four years, and also became a boxing champion!

After his boxing career ended, he travelled around England singing a type of music called Calypso (this music originated in Trinidad and Tobago). He made a home for himself in St Pauls, Bristol. This is where he started his career as an actor and a writer.

Alfred was first on stage at the Bristol Arts Centre, where he played the Nigerian Officer Orara in *The Little Mrs Foster Show*. He made other appearances and did a lot of performing and writing for film, radio, television, and theatre.

Alfred Fagon working with actors at a rehearsal.

A lot of what Alfred wrote was based on his own experiences and the people he saw and met in St Pauls. One of his plays, called *11 Josephine House,* was set in Bristol and was about the different problems many Caribbean people faced when they brought their culture to England. Alfred's last play was called *Lonely Cowboy.* This play was set in Brixton, London and was all about the experiences of the young, Black characters. Alfred Fagon also wrote poetry, including a collection of poems called *Waterwell.*

A statue celebrating Alfred Fagon in Bristol.

Alfred Fagon made a large impact on the arts in Bristol and Britain. There is now an award named after him for new, young playwrights, and a statue celebrating him can be found on the corner of Ashley Road and Grosvenor Road in Bristol!

Activity

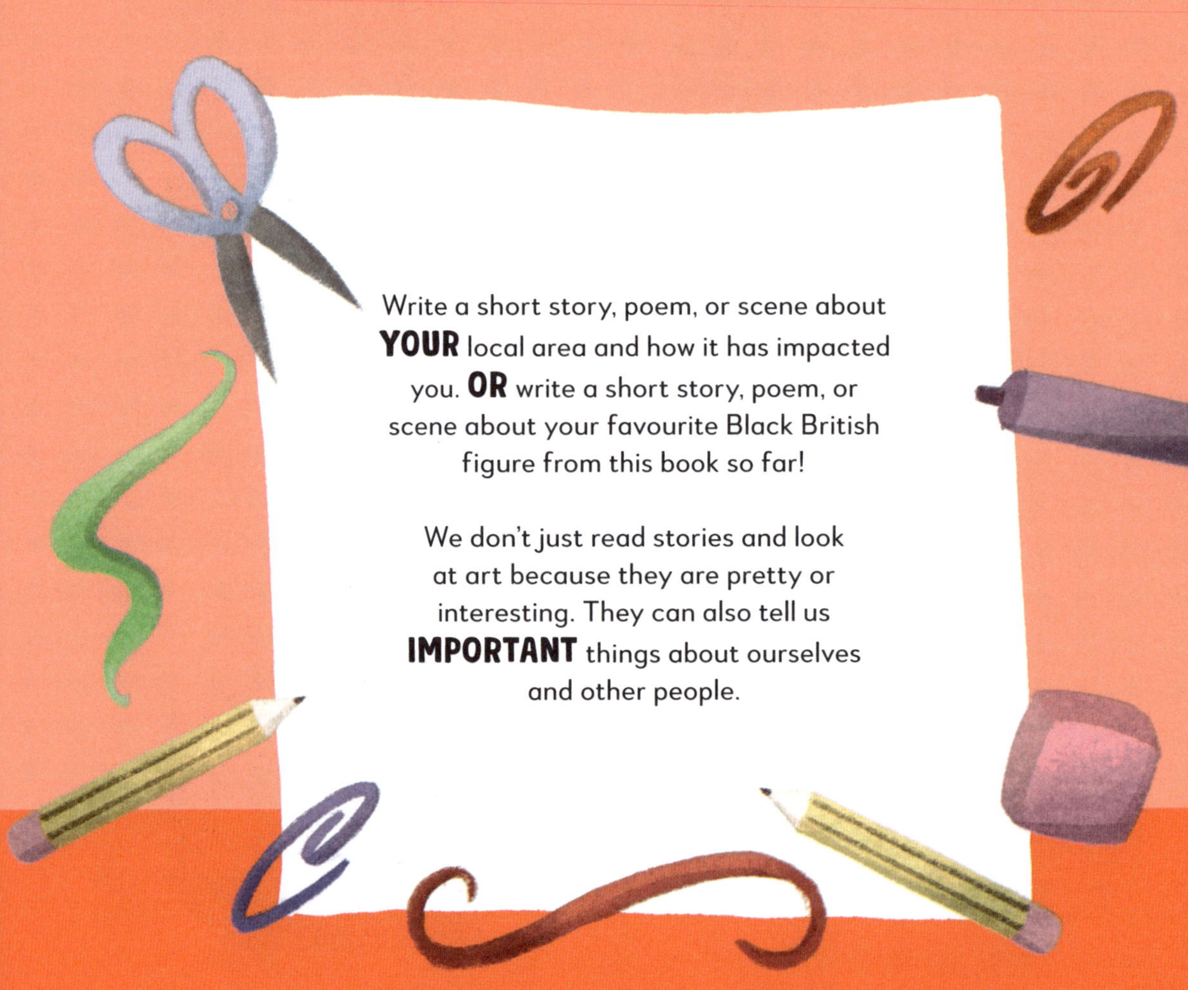

Write a short story, poem, or scene about **YOUR** local area and how it has impacted you. **OR** write a short story, poem, or scene about your favourite Black British figure from this book so far!

We don't just read stories and look at art because they are pretty or interesting. They can also tell us **IMPORTANT** things about ourselves and other people.

Think of all the Black people throughout history who wrote about their experiences, the paintings and photos that show us the different jobs Black people have had over time, and the different music and fun events Black people have created to celebrate themselves.

Princess Campbell (NHS Nurse)

Carmen Beckford (Community Officer)

Alfred Fagon (Boxer/Singer/Actor)

All of this helps us in the present day to understand our history better, learn, and remember others. Your story is **JUST** as important. So get creative and tell your story!

Black British History in Nottingham

We hope you enjoyed exploring Bristol as much as we did! We are now going to take you to Nottingham, where our journey together will end. Like the other places we have explored in this book, Nottingham has historical connections to the slave trade. There were slave auctions (where people bought and sold enslaved Black people) in Goose Gate and the areas around Broadmarsh.

Nottingham was also connected to the Transatlantic Slave Trade because during that time, the slave trade was what helped the city become famous for making lace and tights. In order to make these materials, raw cotton was picked and cleaned by enslaved Black people who worked across the southern states of the US (like Texas) and countries in the Caribbean in the early 19th century (1800s).

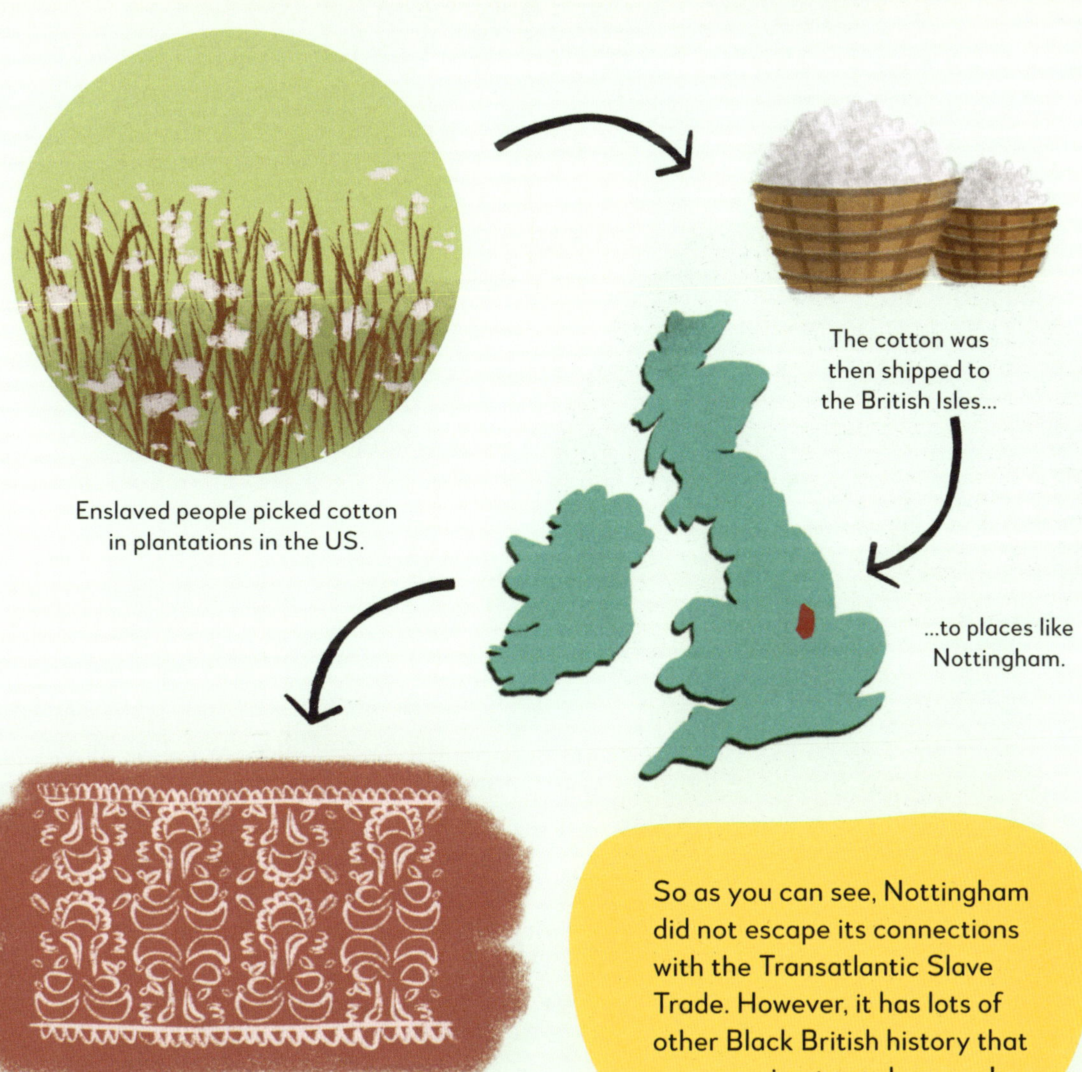

Enslaved people picked cotton in plantations in the US.

The cotton was then shipped to the British Isles...

...to places like Nottingham.

Factory workers in Nottingham then made the cotton into products like lace.

So as you can see, Nottingham did not escape its connections with the Transatlantic Slave Trade. However, it has lots of other Black British history that we are going to explore now!

Nottingham's First Black Businessman

As we have seen, there have been Black people living across Britain for hundreds of years, including in places like Nottingham. However, they weren't always written about, so we don't know much about their lives. The first Black person who lived in Nottingham and was well-recorded by history was a man called George Africanus.

We have looked at a lot of extraordinary people who did big things for their community, but it is always important to notice the ordinary people who made positive impacts in the places they lived. George Africanus is an example of this. He was born in Sierra Leone (a country in West Africa) and came to Wolverhampton when he was a young boy. He had been enslaved and brought to live with a family in Molyneux House. When he lived there, he worked as a servant and was taught to read, write, and do basic maths. As he grew up, George's position changed, and the Molyneux family paid for him to learn to be a brass founder (someone who makes things out of brass).

In 1784, when he was 21 years old, George left the family and moved from Wolverhampton to live in Nottingham. This is where he met his wife, Esther Shaw. George and Esther married at St Peter's Church when George was 25. They lived on Chandlers Lane in the centre of town.

George Africanus worked as a brass founder and his wife as a milliner (a person who makes or sells hats). George also did other kinds of work! He set up an employment agency called "Africanus' Register of Servants", that placed servants with upper class families in Nottingham. He owned property, and he was able to vote in elections. He died when he was 71 in 1834 and was buried in St Mary's churchyard.

IN CONCLUSION...

We will finish our journey here, but we hope that **your journey** through Black British history in **places and spaces** across Britain has **just started!** From universities, clubs, schools, and hospitals, to theatres, docks, and even the streets, we hope this book has shown you that Black British history is **all around you** if you just **look** for it!

To keep **learning** about Black British history, we **encourage** you to look at your town or city and see if there is any **Black British history** to **discover**.

YOU MAY BE SURPRISED AT WHAT YOU FIND OUT!

Glossary

Throughout the book, you may have come across some words you don't know. Check here to find out all the meanings and learn something new! If you are struggling to understand any of the meanings, discuss them with a friend, a parent, a teacher, or someone you know.

Boycott
This is a form of protest where people avoid or stop using something to spread awareness of an injustice.

Campaign
Raise awareness about something or work towards a certain cause.

Civil rights
The principle that every person should be treated equally under law, regardless of who they are.

Colour bar
Until The Race Relations Act of 1965, railway stations, clubs, housing, employers, restaurants, and other public places, were able to discriminate against non-white people. This was known as the colour bar. The Race Relations Act made such racial discrimination in public places against the law.

Inclusive
Not excluding or leaving out other people.

Marginalise
Treat someone as not important, inferior, and not valuable.

MBE
Member of the Order of the British Empire. This is an award that is handed out by the Queen to people who have made a big, positive contribution to British society.

Migrate
Move from one place to another. This is usually when people move from one country to another country to live.

Prejudice
An unfair and usually negative judgement towards an individual or group.

Riot

This is sometimes used to describe events that result in meaningless violence by a crowd.

It is important to remember that the Tiger Bay race riots and the other events that are called "riots" may not actually be riots. A lot of the time in history, uprisings and protests that are related to injustices like racism are called "riots" so victims are seen as troublemakers. Make sure you read the causes of these events carefully, and decide for yourself what you think.

Theory of Evolution

A theory in science, proposed by Charles Darwin, that describes how creatures and living things change and adapt over many generations.

Uprising

This is often used to describe an event where people come together to resist injustice or oppression.

You might also notice that we capitalise the B in Black but not the w in white. Here is the Black Curriculum's note explaining why this is:

We capitalise the B in Black because the word Black in this context reflects a shared sense of identity and, to a certain extent, a community. The case for capitalising Black is also rooted in humanising and uplifting groups that have historically been stripped of this right. White, in this context, does not suffer from the same historical happenings, especially in the context of Britain.

In this book we have focused on Black British history; that's Black history from England, Wales, and Scotland. This is why you'll notice us talking about Britain, which is made up of England, Wales, and Scotland.

We're not referring to the UK, which is made up of Britain and Northern Ireland. Northern Ireland itself has so much Black history that we'd need a whole separate book to cover it properly.

Please note, the maps in this book are not to scale.

Index

Want to find out more about Black British history? Go to www.theblackcurriculum.com to find videos, zines, classroom resources, and more.

If you've enjoyed this book, look out for the other books in this series! *Legacies: Black British Pioneers* and *Migration: Journeys Through Black British History.*

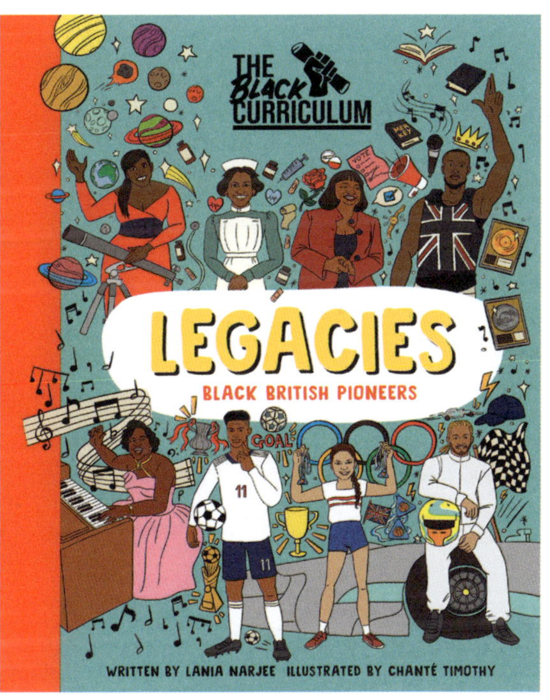

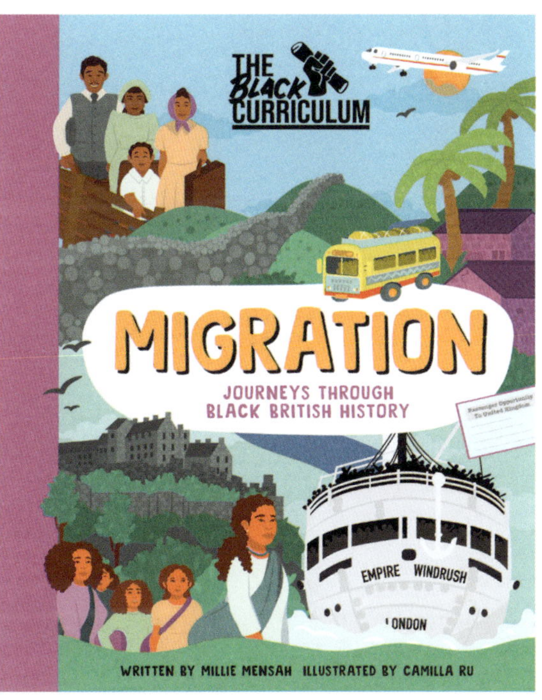

Legacies: Black British Pioneers

Foreword by Lewis Hamilton

Written by Lania Narjee
Illustrated by Chanté Timothy

Migration: Journeys Through Black British History

Foreword by Oghenemaro Itoje

Written by Millie Mensah
Illustrated by Camilla Ru

Project Editor Rosie Peet
Project Art Editor Stefan Georgiou
Senior Acquisitions Editor Katy Flint
Managing Art Editor Vicky Short
Production Editor Siu Yin Chan
Production Controller Louise Minihane
Publishing Director Mark Searle

Written by Melody Triumph
Illustrated by Amanda Quartey

First published in Great Britain in 2022 by Dorling Kindersley Limited
DK, One Embassy Gardens, 8 Viaduct Gardens, London SW11 7BW

The authorised representative in the EEA is Dorling Kindersley Verlag GmbH. Arnulfstr. 124, 80636 Munich, Germany

10 9 8 7 6 5 4 3 2
002–328149–Aug/2022

A CIP catalogue record for this book is available from the British Library.
ISBN: 978-0-2415-5282-7

Printed in the UK

The publisher would like to thank Chima Itabor for providing the authenticity read; Victoria Armstrong, Lisa Gillespie, and Julia March at DK for editorial support; and Ilhan Rayen Awed and Saffa Khalil at The Black Curriculum.

For the curious

www.dk.com

This book was made with Forest Stewardship Council ™ certified paper– one small step in DK's commitment to a sustainable future. For more information go to www.dk.com/our-green-pledge

GLASSFORD STREET

N
W E
S

N
W E
S

N
W E
S

INGRAM STREET